JOHN MILNE

The Case of the Lonely Lady

HEINEMANN

Series Editor: John Milne

The Heinemann Guided Readers provide a choice of enjoyable reading material for learners of English. The series is published at five levels – Starter, Beginner, Elementary, Intermediate and Upper. At **Intermediate Level**, the control of content and language has the following main features:

Information Control
Information which is vital to the understanding of the story is presented in an easily assimilated manner and is repeated when necessary. Difficult allusion and metaphor are avoided and cultural backgrounds are made explicit.

Structure Control
Most of the structures used in the Readers will be familiar to students who have completed an elementary course of English. Other grammatical features may occur, but their use is made clear through context and reinforcement. This ensures that the reading, as well as being enjoyable, provides a continual learning situation for the students. Sentences are limited in most cases to a maximum of three clauses and within sentences there is a balanced use of adverbial and adjectival phrases. Great care is taken with pronoun reference.

Vocabulary Control
There is a basic vocabulary of approximately 1,600 words. Help is given to the students in the form of illustrations, which are closely related to the text.

Glossary
Some difficult words and phrases in this book are important for understanding the story. Some of these words are explained in the story, some are shown in the pictures, and others are marked with a number like this . . .[3] Words with a number are explained in the Glossary on page 59.

Contents

The People in This Story

Nancy Roberts is forty-six years old. For many years she and her family lived in India. They came to live in England in 1970. Now her parents are dead. Nancy is a quiet and lonely woman.

Henry Jones is in his late forties. He is a widower. His wife died a year ago.

Isobel Jones is about the same age as Nancy Roberts. She lives with her brother Henry Jones, in a small town near London.

Terry Mason used to work in an office. But he did not like his job. He always wanted to become a detective. Then one day Terry's uncle died and left him some money. Now Terry Mason is a private investigator.

Sheila Williams has known Terry Mason for many years. Sheila works in an estate agent's office.

Bill Evans is a milkman. He delivers milk to people's houses early every day. He drives a milkfloat.
Tom Matthews is thirteen years old. He is a newspaper boy. He delivers papers to people's houses early every day.

Bob Wilkinson is a friend of Terry's. He works in a building society.
Gordon Burgess is a friend of Terry's. He works for the Town Council.

Cheltenham
Gloucester
LONDON
Cardiff
Bristol
Bath
Beckenham
Canterbury
Folkestone • Dover
Southampton Brighton
Bournemouth
Hastings
Eastbourne
Beachy Head

Map of South-East England

1

A Lonely Woman

Nancy Roberts was born in 1943. Her father worked in an import/export company in Bombay in India. Nancy had no brothers or sisters and she was always a lonely girl. She went to school in India. Most of the other girls at her school were the daughters of British people who worked in India.

Nancy made some friends at school. When Nancy left school, she wrote letters to her friends. But, as time passed, her friends got married or went to live in England. They forgot about Nancy and she received fewer and fewer letters.

The last letter Nancy received was from Julie Summers. In her letter, Julie said she had got married and was going to live in England with her husband. They were going to live in Eastbourne on the south coast. Julie promised to write again when she knew their new address in Eastbourne. But Julie never wrote again and Nancy received no more letters.

When Nancy's father retired[1] in 1970, he and his wife came to England and bought a house in Cheltenham. Nancy was twenty-seven years old. She lived a quiet life with her parents and had no friends.

Nancy was forty-two when her mother died. Her father died four years later. Nancy was now alone at the age of forty-six. She did not know what to do. She did not need to work. Both her parents had left[2] her money. Nancy was not a rich woman. But she had enough money to live on for the rest of her life.

Nancy decided she must have a holiday. But where could she go? What could she do? She thought of going back to India. Perhaps she could find some of her old school friends again. But what would she do if she did not find anyone? How lonely it would be travelling on her own!

Then she remembered the last letter from Julie Summers. Julie had said that she was going to live in Eastbourne. Eastbourne was a holiday resort[3], wasn't it? Why not go there for a holiday?

Nancy's father had died in September and it was now October. The weather was dry and bright. Nancy decided to have a holiday in Eastbourne. She might be lucky. She might meet Julie Summers.

Nancy locked up the lonely house in Cheltenham and went to stay in a small hotel in Eastbourne. She was going to stay there for the winter.

Nancy was forty-six years old, but she was a good-looking woman. She might not meet Julie Summers. But she might meet someone she could make friends with. Perhaps – perhaps – but Nancy knew that her dreams never came true. She was afraid that she was going to be lonely for the rest of her life.

2

Nancy Makes Friends

But Nancy did make friends in the small hotel in Eastbourne. First, she made friends with Isobel Jones. Isobel was about the same age as Nancy, perhaps a little older. Nancy saw that Isobel was also alone. They sat at the same table one morning at breakfast and began to talk to each other. Nancy thought Isobel was a nice, friendly person.

After breakfast, Isobel said, 'Why don't we go for a walk together? We could go up to the top of Beachy Head. The views over the Channel are beautiful.'

Nancy quickly agreed and the two began their walk up to the top of Beachy Head.

'Are you staying here long?' Nancy asked Isobel.

'I don't know,' replied Isobel. 'I'm waiting for my brother, Henry. Henry has some business to do in Brighton. He'll be coming here in a few days. Then we'll decide whether to stay here or go somewhere else.'

What a pity, thought Nancy to herself. I've just made a friend and now I'm going to lose her.

But Nancy did not lose her friend. When Henry arrived, he and his sister decided to stay in Eastbourne. And Henry went with his sister and Nancy on their long morning walks up to Beachy Head and along the high cliffs.

Henry Jones was in his forties. He had a large moustache which Nancy did not think was very attractive. And his hair was thin at the front. In fact, he was almost bald. But he was amusing and knew lots of funny stories. Time passed quickly when Henry Jones was with the two ladies.

Nancy told Isobel and Henry everything about herself. She told them about her life in India – about the death of her mother and father – about the lonely house in Cheltenham.

One morning, Henry came down alone to breakfast. He had a message for Nancy.

'I'm afraid Isobel is not well today. She has a cold,' he said. 'We won't be able to have our walk together.'

'What a pity,' said Nancy. 'Shall I go up to her room and see her?'

'I think she wants to sleep,' replied Henry.

Nancy did not know what to say. She was going to be on her own again. And she had enjoyed being with her new friends. She was a shy[4] woman, but she decided she had to do something. She looked at Henry and said, 'It's a beautiful day. We should not stay indoors. Perhaps we could go for a walk together?'

Henry, Isobel and Nancy went on long walks along the high cliffs.

That was how their love affair[5] started. Isobel's cold got worse and she had to stay in her room. Henry and Nancy often went for a walk together in the morning after breakfast. They walked up to the top of the cliffs and stood looking out over the Channel towards France.

3

Christmas Day

The hotel became busier before Christmas. Isobel's cold was better and she was able to come downstairs for the Christmas party.

Nancy had never felt so happy. She sat with Henry and Isobel and the three of them ate a delicious meal and drank champagne.

After the meal, Isobel said she was tired. She went back to her room. The other guests all went out for a walk. Nancy and Henry were left alone.

Henry began to speak about himself and his life. He had been married. He had lived with his wife in Beckenham, a small town about nine miles from London.

'Isobel lived with us,' Henry said.

'Where is your wife now?' asked Nancy.

'She died last summer,' replied Henry. 'Now Isobel and I are alone.'

Nancy and Henry sat together in the sitting-room as it grew dark. Henry began to speak slowly and quietly.

'We will soon be going back to our empty house in Beckenham,' he said. 'You know that I have become very fond of you, Nancy. I have been thinking . . . I mean Isobel and I have been talking together . . .'

Nancy sat in silence. What was Henry trying to say?

10

'Will you come with us?' he asked suddenly.

'What do you mean?'

'Will you marry me and come back with us to Beckenham?'

Nancy agreed. She was very happy. She was never going to be alone again!

'But I don't want you to tell anyone that we are engaged,' said Henry. 'Isobel must be the first one to know.'

4

A Quiet Wedding

The next day, Isobel felt much better. But Henry did not feel well. He had caught Isobel's cold. He stayed in his room. Isobel and Nancy had a long walk together.

'Henry told me the good news this morning,' Isobel said. 'I'm sure the three of us will be very happy together.'

Nancy agreed.

'Has Henry told you that he has some business to do in Hastings?' asked Isobel.

'No,' said Nancy in surprise.

'He was thinking so much of you that he forgot all about his business,' said Isobel. 'He has to leave Eastbourne in a few days and go to Hastings.'

'Perhaps we could go with him,' said Nancy. 'We could all go together.'

'That's a wonderful idea,' said Isobel. 'But it will be better if Henry goes alone to Hastings to finish his business. Then we can meet him there after a week. I don't think we need to tell anyone here in the hotel about our plans, do we? We don't know any of them well. They are all strangers, aren't they?'

Nancy agreed.

11

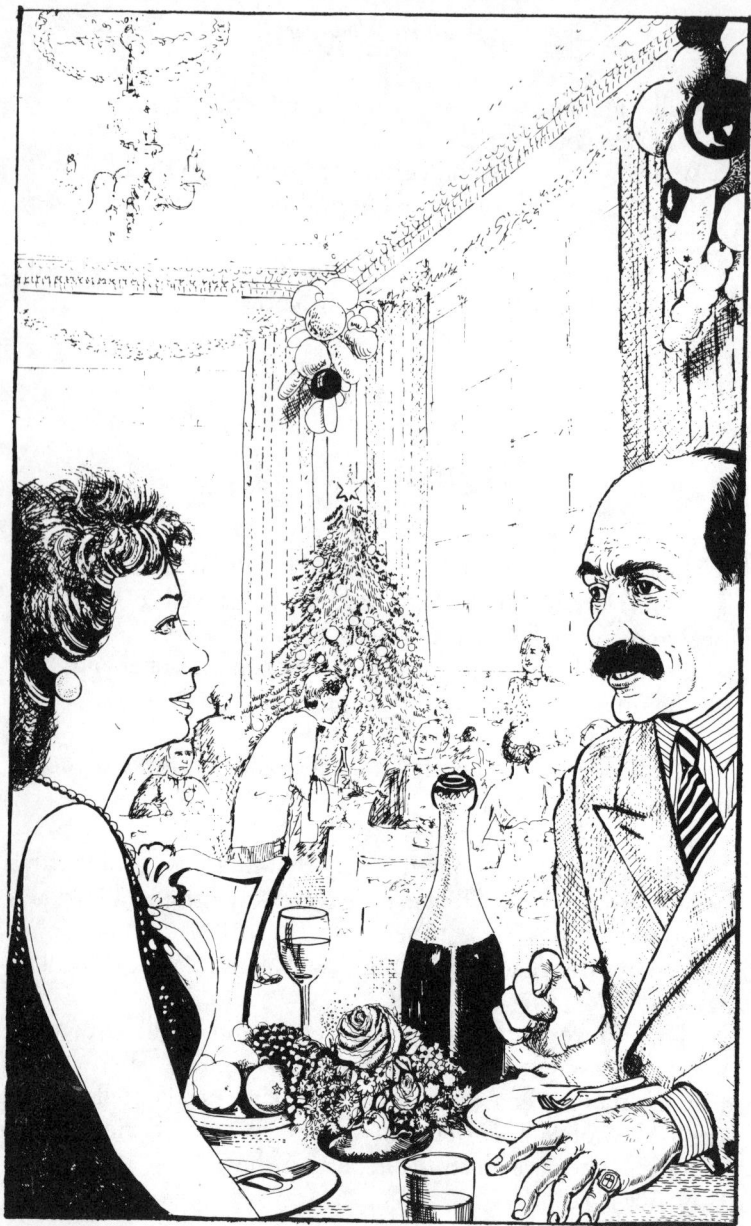

'Will you marry me and come back with us to Beckenham?'

'I'll tell the hotel manager that I am going back to Cheltenham,' she said. 'Then he won't know anything about our plans.'

So it was all arranged. First, Henry went alone to Hastings. Nancy and Isobel left Eastbourne a week later.

When Isobel and Nancy arrived in Hastings, Henry was waiting for them at the railway station. He had some bad news. The hotel he was staying in was full. But he had arranged for them to stay in another hotel not far away.

Nancy did not see much of Henry in Hastings. He had a lot to do. He had some business to finish and he had to arrange the wedding. It was January and the weather was wet and cold. Isobel often did not feel well and stayed in her bedroom. Nancy spent most of the time alone, reading.

At last Henry's business was finished and all the arrangements for the wedding were made. Nancy and Henry were married quietly[6] in a registry office[7]. The only witnesses[8] were Isobel and a man who cleaned the registry office. After they had signed the register, Nancy, Henry and Isobel went to catch a train to Beckenham.

It had been a quiet wedding – a very quiet wedding.

5

Nancy is a Prisoner

As soon as they got off the train at Beckenham, Henry told Nancy he had some shopping to do. Nancy and Isobel got into a taxi. They got out of the taxi at the corner of a street. Henry arrived a few moments later. He came in another taxi but he had not got any shopping with him.

Nancy and Henry were married quietly in a registry office.

They walked quickly down a quiet, empty street, carrying their heavy suitcases. They stopped at a large, dark house. Number 12 was painted on the gate. Tall, thick bushes grew in the small garden at the front of the house. Henry quickly opened the door and they went in.

They went downstairs to a large kitchen. Nancy sat down at the kitchen table.

'I'm going upstairs to get our rooms ready,' Isobel said to Nancy. 'Henry will make us all some hot coffee.'

Isobel went upstairs and Henry made the coffee. After Nancy drank the coffee, she felt sleepy.

'You're tired after the long journey,' Nancy heard Henry saying. 'I'll help you upstairs to bed.'

When Nancy woke up, she was lying in a bed in a strange room. It was dark and she did not know where she was. She felt tired and went back to sleep again.

When she woke up again, it was morning. Isobel came into the room with breakfast on a tray.

'You're not well,' said Isobel. 'You must lie here quietly until you are better. I have brought some orange juice for you to drink.'

'Where's Henry?' Nancy asked.

'He has some business in the town today,' Isobel replied. 'He'll come up and see you as soon as he gets back.'

But Henry did not come up to see her. It was Isobel who came back with some lunch. After lunch, Isobel helped Nancy to get out of bed and go to the bathroom.

'I feel very strange,' said Nancy. 'I think I am ill.'

'Yes, you are ill,' said Isobel. 'But you'll soon get better.'

'Where's Henry?' Nancy asked again.

'He'll be here soon,' Isobel replied. But Henry did not come. It was Isobel who brought her supper. And after supper, Nancy again felt tired and went back to sleep.

The next morning, Nancy woke up very early. She felt better

15

and got out of bed. She walked slowly to the window. She saw that she was in an upstairs bedroom, high above the street. Nancy tried to open the window, but it was locked. She walked slowly to the door. It was locked too. There was another door in the bedroom. It was not locked. It led into the bathroom. There was a window in the bathroom, but it was high up in the ceiling. There was no way out of the bedroom.

Nancy was worried. Why was the door locked? Why hadn't Henry come to see her? Nancy felt afraid. She was alone, locked in a large, empty house. What were Henry and Isobel planning to do? Were they planning to steal her money? After the wedding, Henry had asked Nancy to sign some papers. He had told her the papers were for the wedding. Nancy had not read the papers carefully. What had she signed? Had she given all her money away?

Nancy realised what a fool she had been. She had told the manager at the hotel in Eastbourne that she was going back to Cheltenham. She had not said anything about going with Henry and Isobel. She had not told anyone that she and Henry were going to get married.

In Hastings, Nancy had not stayed at the same hotel as Henry. She had spent most of the time alone in her room and had not spoken to anyone. Then they had got married quietly in a registry office. The only witnesses were Isobel and the cleaner. No one knew where they had come from. No one knew where they were going to.

What a terrible fool she had been!

The days passed and Nancy was kept locked in the upstairs bedroom. She did not see Henry again. Nancy was sure that Isobel was trying to poison[9] her. She tried not to drink or eat anything Isobel brought to her. There was water in the bathroom. But she often felt hungry and had to eat something.

The house was always quiet. No visitors came to the house. A milkman[10] passed by the house early every morning. Nancy could not see him from the upstairs window, but she could hear the noise of his milkfloat. And there was a paperboy who went past soon after the milkman. Again, Nancy could not see him, but she could hear him whistling as he went by. But the milkman never stopped to leave milk at the door of Number 12. The paperboy never pushed a paper through the letterbox.

Every time Isobel came into the bedroom, Nancy asked her questions.

'Why have you locked me in here? What's happening?'

But Nancy never got any answers to her questions. Isobel came into the room and left again without speaking.

Once, Nancy had a chance to let someone know that she was locked in the bedroom. She heard someone coming up the stairs. She knew that the footsteps were not Isobel's. It was Henry and there was someone with him.

Nancy climbed slowly out of the bed and walked over to the locked door. She put her ear against the wooden door and listened. She heard a woman's voice. It was the voice of a young woman and she was asking questions. Henry was answering. Then the voices came nearer.

'You don't need to see into this room,' said Henry. 'It's the same as the other two rooms on this floor[11]. I've left the key somewhere and I can't find it.'

Nancy suddenly knew what was happening. Henry Jones was planning to sell the house.

Nancy was going to be murdered. Her body was going to be hidden somewhere – buried in the garden. Then Henry Jones and his sister would leave town. Nancy's body would never be found.

Nancy started to beat on the door with her hands. She shouted loudly, 'Help me! Help me!' But there was no reply. She heard the footsteps going down the stairs. She was once again left alone in the locked room at the top of the large, empty house.

17

6

Terry Mason — Private Investigator

On Monday, 1st February, Terry Mason left his office at half past five. Before he left the office, he switched on the answering machine of his telephone. It was the first time he had switched on the answering machine and he hoped it would work. He hoped there would be a message for him when he came back to the office the next morning.

As he locked the office door, he read the notice which had been put there that morning.

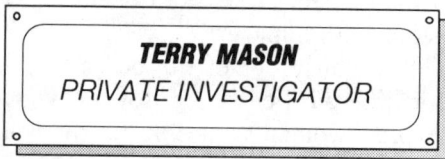

TERRY MASON
PRIVATE INVESTIGATOR

Terry smiled to himself as he went down the stairs. At last he was a private investigator.

It was a cold February evening. But Terry felt happy as he walked towards his favourite pub, The Eight Bells. He knew his friend, Sheila Williams, would be waiting for him. The two of them often had a drink together in the evening.

Sheila and Terry had gone to school together. They had both started work at the same time. Terry got a job in the South-Eastern Building Society[12]. And Sheila got a job in an estate agent's[13] office – Bedford and Company. Sheila liked her work. She liked helping people to buy and sell their houses.

But Terry did not like his job in the building society. He was often bored. He wanted to do something more exciting.

Terry's favourite films and books were about detectives. He always watched detective films on TV. His favourite films were the films about Perry Mason. Perry Mason was an American lawyer who was also a detective. Terry Mason – Perry Mason – the names sounded the same. Perhaps it was because the names sounded the same that Terry dreamed of becoming a detective!

When there wasn't a good film on TV, Terry read detective stories. He had read them all – the adventures of Sherlock Holmes – the adventures of Hercule Poirot – the adventures of Philip Marlowe. Terry did not want to work all his life in a building society office. He wanted to become a detective. He wanted to become like his hero – Perry Mason.

A few weeks before Christmas, Terry got a letter from a solicitor[14] in London. The letter told Terry that an uncle had died and left Terry ten thousand pounds. Terry knew what he was going to do. He was going to use the money to do something he had always wanted to do. He was going to become a detective – a private investigator.

When Terry had told Sheila about his plan, she thought he was mad.

'Beckenham is too small a place for a private investigator,' Sheila told him. 'No one will go to a private investigator in a small place like this. I know everybody likes you in Beckenham. I know you are popular. But if anyone in Beckenham wants a private investigator, they'll go to London. They won't come to you.'

But Terry would not listen. He rented[15] an office. He rented a telephone and an answering machine. And he put an advert[16] in the paper:

PRIVATE INVESTIGATOR
All enquiries undertaken in strictest confidence
RING 01 658 2786

And he had a card printed:

TERRY MASON
PRIVATE INVESTIGATOR
01 658 2786

Terry reached The Eight Bells at six o'clock. The pub was always busy at that time in the evening. When Terry came through the door, there was a cheer from the crowd of young people in the bar.

'Here comes Sherlock Holmes!' someone shouted. And there was a laugh and a loud cheer.

'Any murders today?' Sheila asked Terry when he sat down at the table beside her.

Terry did not reply. He picked up his drink and began to drink it slowly.

'Something strange happened to me today,' said Sheila.

'What happened?' asked Terry.

'You know those houses in Oakwood Avenue?'

'You mean the large houses in the quiet road behind the park?'

'That's right,' said Sheila. 'I went to look at one of them today – Number 12. The man who owns it is called Mr Jones. He said his wife bought it a few years ago. Now he wants to sell it. He came into the office late on Friday afternoon and we arranged a meeting. I arranged to go there at three o'clock this afternoon. But I made a mistake and I got there at two.

'I said I was sorry for coming so early. Mr Jones let me in, but he was not happy about me arriving early. He showed me round the house[17], but he seemed all the time to be listening for something.'

'Is that all?' asked Terry with a laugh.

'No, there's more,' replied Sheila. 'There are three rooms on the top floor. He showed me into two of the rooms. Then he said the third door was locked and he could not find the key. So we started to go back down the stairs. Then I heard it.'

'Heard what?'

'A knocking on the door and a voice. Someone was calling for help. It was difficult to hear, but I am sure I heard it.'

'What did you do?' asked Terry, who was now becoming interested in Sheila's story.

'I did nothing,' replied Sheila. 'I pretended[18] that I had heard nothing. I'm sure Mr Jones thinks that I heard nothing.'

'It may be easily explained,' said Terry.

'What's the explanation, then, Mr Private Investigator?'

'Mr Jones has a son or a daughter who had behaved badly. The boy or the girl had been locked in the room as a punishment.'

'Mr Jones lives with his sister,' replied Sheila. 'He told me that his wife died when they were on holiday. And I'm sure that it was a woman's voice – not a child's voice.'

Terry thought for a few moments.

'All right,' he said. 'I agree with you. It is interesting. This will be my first case[19]. But I'm sure that it will be easily explained.'

7
Terry Goes Running

The next morning, Sheila typed a letter and posted it to 12 Oakwood Avenue.

> *Bedford and Company*
> *621 High Street*
> *Beckenham*
> *Kent*

Dear Mr Jones,

A Mr Smith has phoned us. He is interested in buying your house. Would you please let me know when I can come with Mr Smith and show him round the house.

Yours sincerely,

Sheila

Sheila Williams

On Friday, Sheila received a reply. Mr Jones was ready to meet Miss Williams and Mr Smith the following Monday afternoon at three o'clock. Would Miss Williams please make sure she came at the exact time?

On Friday evening, Sheila and Terry met in The Eight Bells. 'You've got an appointment on Monday afternoon, Mr Smith,' said Sheila with a laugh. 'Mr Jones is ready to meet us both at three o'clock – but it must be at three o'clock exactly!'

The next day, Saturday, it was cold and wet. But Terry got up early and left the house wearing his tracksuit and his trainers. He was going running. He ran along through the wet streets to

Oakwood Avenue. The rain was dripping from the trees in front of the houses.

Terry stopped in front of Number 12. He knelt down and pretended to tie up his trainers. Number 12 looked empty. There were thick bushes in front of the house. There was grass growing on the path up to the front door. All the windows were covered with dark curtains.

Terry ran slowly along Oakwood Avenue. He saw Bill Evans, the milkman, standing beside his milkfloat.

'Morning, Bill,' said Terry.

'Morning, Terry,' said Bill. 'What are you doing out here on a wet morning like this? Looking for a murderer?'

Terry laughed. Everyone in Beckenham knew about him. They had all read his advert in the paper.

'Who lives at Number 12?' Terry asked Bill.

'Don't know. I haven't seen anyone going in or out for months. Miss Peters used to live there. But last summer she went somewhere on holiday. Hastings, I think. Or was it Eastbourne? I'm not sure. I heard she'd got married. She never came back. The house has been empty ever since.'

'How old was Miss Peters?'

'Oh, about forty, I think. But quite a good-looking lady. I wasn't surprised when I heard she'd got married. That's all I know about Number 12. But here's Tom Matthews. He delivers newspapers around here. He may be able to tell you more.'

But Tom Matthews could not tell Terry anything more about Number 12. Tom had never delivered any newspapers there and he had never seen anyone come out or go in. Tom thought the house was empty.

Terry ran slowly back home. He had learnt very little about Mr Jones of Number 12. But he had learnt one thing. Sheila had said that Mr Jones was not married. He lived with his sister. So what had happened to Miss Peters? She had lived at Number 12 until last summer. What had happened to her?

Terry ran slowly along Oakwood Avenue.

8

Terry Needs Some Information

On Saturday afternoon, Terry was once again out in the rain. He was the referee at the football matches played by the Beckenham Youth Team. He ran up and down the field getting wetter and wetter. He was glad when it was time to blow the final whistle.

While he was having a hot shower, he had to listen to more jokes.

'Caught any spies yet?' asked one young man. And everyone laughed.

And it was the same in The Eight Bells in the evening.

'Where's your pipe, Sherlock Holmes?' someone shouted. Everyone laughed loudly.

Terry sat down and had a quiet talk with Sheila. He told her what he had learnt from Bill Evans, the milkman.

'That's very interesting,' said Sheila. 'If Miss Peters was the owner of the house, why is Mr Henry Jones selling it? And he told me he was not married. He said he lives with his sister.'

'Are we sure of that?' asked Terry. 'You haven't seen the sister, have you?'

'I didn't see anyone at Number 12 except Mr Jones. But I did hear that knocking and the voice coming from the upstairs bedroom.'

'Can we find out if there's a mortgage[20] on the house?' said Terry. 'If there is a mortgage, we can find out who is the owner of the house. Perhaps Bob Wilkinson can help us.'

Bob Wilkinson was a friend of Terry's. Bob worked in the South-Eastern Building Society where Terry had worked. Bob was standing by the bar having a drink. Terry called him over.

'Can you help me?' Terry asked Bob. 'I need some information about Number 12 Oakwood Avenue. Is there any way you can find out if there's a mortgage on the house?'

'That's easy if there's a mortgage with our company,' replied Bob. 'But, of course, such information is confidential[21]. I should not tell anyone.'

'But you *can* help me, can't you?' Terry asked Bob. Bob promised to help Terry if he could.

9

Mr Jones Becomes Angry

Terry phoned Bob Wilkinson at midday on Monday.
'There's a mortgage on Number 12 Oakwood Avenue,' Bob told Terry. 'The owner was a Miss Peters. But she signed a paper last October giving the house to her husband, Mr Henry Jones. So Mr Jones is now the owner.'

'Thanks a lot, Bob. I won't forget your help.'

Terry told Sheila what he had learnt from Bob Wilkinson.

'It's very strange,' said Terry. 'Mr Jones told you he wasn't married. So where is Miss Peters now?'

'Locked up in the upstairs bedroom?' said Sheila.

'It is getting more and more interesting. You could be right. Perhaps he has locked his wife up in the bedroom. And he is trying to sell the house and run away with the money.'

On Monday afternoon, Sheila drove Terry to 12 Oakwood Avenue. They were at the door at three o'clock exactly. Terry was wearing his father's jacket and trousers and he had put some white powder on his hair. Terry, or Mr Smith, looked like a man over the age of forty.

As soon as Sheila knocked on the door, it opened. Mr Jones must have been waiting behind the door for them to arrive. Mr Jones showed them round the rooms on the ground floor. They looked first at the sitting-room.

'Look how the sun shines into the sitting-room in the afternoon,' said Sheila. 'It is a winter afternoon, but it's bright and sunny in here.'

Terry did not think it was bright and sunny. He thought it was cold and dark. But he knew Sheila was doing her job. She wanted to make Mr Jones believe that she was trying to sell his house.

'We'll look at the upstairs rooms first,' Mr Jones told them. 'Then later we'll go downstairs and look at the kitchen and the cellars.'

Mr Jones showed them the bedrooms on the second floor. Then he took them up to the bedrooms on the top floor. The door of the three bedrooms on the top floor were open.

'You found the key to this room?' Sheila asked.

'Yes,' said Mr Jones.

Sheila went into the room and looked around.

'Where does that door go?' she asked Mr Jones.

'This bedroom has its own bathroom,' he replied.

Mr Jones opened the bathroom door and Sheila followed him inside. Mr Jones suddenly looked round.

'Where's Mr Smith?' he asked Sheila.

'Perhaps he has gone to look at the other bedrooms,' replied Sheila.

Mr Jones hurried out and looked into the other bedrooms. Sheila was left alone. She quickly went over to the bed and turned down the sheets. She felt them with her hand. They were warm.

'Mr Smith! Mr Smith!' Mr Jones shouted angrily as he ran down the stairs after Terry.

He found Terry in the hallway.

'I don't want you walking round my house on your own!' said Mr Jones angrily.

Then he took them up to the bedrooms on the top floor.

'I wanted to look at the sitting-room again,' said Terry. 'But you have locked the door.'

'Get out of my house, both of you!' shouted Mr Jones, his face becoming red with anger. 'This is my house! I have not sold this house yet. You cannot walk round the house as you please.'

Mr Jones walked to the front door and opened it.

'Get out and don't come back. I will not be using your estate agency, Miss Williams. I will get another company to sell this house.'

10

Henry Disagrees with Isobel

As soon as he had shut the front door, Henry Jones went and knocked on the door of the sitting-room. The door opened and Isobel immediately began to argue with Henry.

'Someone tried to come into this room,' she said. 'And I am sure that they saw that the door was locked on the inside. Let's forget this house and sell her house in Cheltenham. That will be much easier.'

'Don't be a fool,' he shouted angrily. 'We can't leave an empty house. Someone will become suspicious[22]. They'll begin to ask questions about the owner. Where is Miss Peters? Where has she gone?'

'We must sell this house. We have always done that in the past. We can't leave this town until we have sold the house.'

'But we can't do that until this one has gone,' said Isobel, pointing at Nancy who was lying on a sofa.

'All right,' agreed Henry. 'Let's get her upstairs now. Come on. Stand up!' he shouted at Nancy.

'I haven't killed her. They die, but I don't kill them.'

But Nancy did not hear him. She was asleep. Henry had crushed a lot of morphine tablets[23] into the orange juice Isobel had given her to drink.

'Perhaps she's dead,' said Isobel. 'You've given her too much morphine and you've killed her.'

'I haven't killed her,' Henry shouted with anger. 'I never kill people. They die, but I don't kill them.'

Isobel did not argue with Henry about this. All the women had died. They had not been killed.

Isobel and Henry lifted Nancy and carried her up the stairs. They threw her down on the bed and left her in the locked bedroom.

'She'll be all right here,' said Henry. 'Perhaps, by morning, she'll be gone. Then we can sell this house and get as far away from here as possible.'

11

Terry Keeps a Secret

Sheila and Terry got into the car and drove off.

'Where are we going?' asked Sheila.

'Let's go to Toni's,' replied Terry. 'We have a lot to talk about. I'm sure there is something strange about Number 12 Oakwood Avenue. I think this is my first case.'

Toni's was their favourite café. They often met there for lunch. They were well-known in the café. The café was almost empty, but Terry had to listen to another joke about private investigators.

Mary, one of the girls who worked in the café, came up to Terry.

31

'I was followed home last night by a tall man with a long beard,' she said. 'I'm frightened. Will you walk home with me tonight?'

'If Terry is going to walk home with you, then I am coming too,' said Sheila. And Mary started to laugh.

'Bring us two coffees,' said Terry. 'I've heard enough jokes about private investigators.'

'Well, what do you think?' Sheila asked Terry.

'There is something strange about that house,' said Terry. 'When I found that the door into the sitting-room was locked, I bent down and tried to look through the keyhole. But I couldn't see into the room. The key was in the lock. The door had been locked on the inside. There was someone in the sitting-room.'

'And the sheets on the bed in the upstairs bedroom were warm,' said Sheila. 'Someone had been lying in that bed.'

'I know what they did,' said Terry. 'They moved the person in the bedroom down to the kitchen before we arrived. Then, while we were upstairs, they moved the person from the kitchen up to the sitting-room and locked the door. They were planning to take the woman back upstairs to the bedroom while we were downstairs in the kitchen. I must look into that upstairs bedroom without Jones seeing me.'

'But how will you do it?' asked Sheila. 'Are you going to break into the house at night? You'll be arrested[24]. You'll be the criminal – not Mr Jones!'

'I've got an idea,' said Terry suddenly. 'I remember reading about it in a detective story. It told you how to look into an upstairs bedroom window!'

'But this is real life,' said Sheila, 'it's not a story. Things don't happen in real life the way they do in stories.'

'I'll have a try anyway,' said Terry.

'What are you going to do?'

'I'm not going to tell you,' replied Terry. 'You'll laugh at me – and I don't want to be laughed at any more. I'm going back to my

32

office now. Perhaps there's a message on the answering machine for me. Someone may have read my advert. They may be looking for a detective!'

Sheila laughed and got into the car and drove back to the estate agency office on the High Street.

12

Mr Jones Does Some Gardening

When Terry got back to the office, there were no messages waiting for him on the answering machine. Perhaps Sheila was right. Perhaps he had made a mistake. Beckenham was a small place. No one would ever want a private investigator in Beckenham.

Then Terry thought about 12 Oakwood Avenue. Perhaps he and Sheila were wrong about Mr Jones. There were many strange people in the world. They did many strange things, but not all of them were criminals. Perhaps he should forget about the house at 12 Oakwood Avenue.

He would have to wait for someone to come through the door or call him on the telephone. It was foolish to go looking for people who might not want or need a private investigator.

As he was leaving the office, there were sounds of footsteps on the stairs. He had two visitors! Bill Evans, the milkman, and Tom Matthews, the newspaper boy.

'What can I do for you two?' asked Terry.

'Tom's got something to tell you,' said Bill. 'Come on Tom, don't be afraid. Tell Terry what you saw this morning.'

'There's a footpath,' Tom began, 'that goes behind the houses

33

from Oakwood Avenue to Manor Park Road. The path goes beside the garden of Number 12 Oakwood Avenue. The garden fence of Number 12 has broken in some places. It's easy to see through it.

'When I was looking through the garden fence, a man started to shout at me. He told me that the garden was private. And ordered me to go away.'

'What did the man look like?' asked Terry.

'An old man – over forty – with a large moustache. And he's almost bald.'

'Yes,' said Terry, 'that's Mr Jones. He lives at Number 12.'

'But that's not all,' said Bill Evans. 'Tell Terry what the man was doing.'

'He was digging a deep hole under some bushes,' said Tom.

'Perhaps he was doing some work in the garden,' said Terry.

'It didn't look like he was working in the garden,' said Tom. 'He was digging a deep hole – a hole deep enough to bury someone in. It looked like he was digging a grave.'

'Tom reads all the murder stories in the newspapers,' said Bill. 'I knew you were interested in Number 12. So I thought we'd better come and tell you what Tom had seen.'

Terry thanked Bill and Tom.

'I'm sure that there's something strange going on at Number 12,' he said.

'If you need any more help, you know where to find us,' said Bill. 'I'm always at home in the afternoon and Tom finishes school at a quarter to four.'

Terry knew now what he was going to do. He was going to have a look in the upstairs bedroom at Number 12. And he would have a look into the garden at the same time.

Terry locked up the office and went to see Gordon Burgess. Gordon Burgess was a friend who worked for the Town Council.

'He was digging a deep hole under some bushes.'

13

High in the Sky

Terry asked Gordon Burgess to help him.

'I want to have a look in an upstairs bedroom at 12 Oakwood Avenue,' Terry told Gordon. 'And you can help me.'

'How can I help you?' asked Gordon.

'You're in charge of street lighting maintenance[25], aren't you?'

'Yes, I am,' said Gordon.

'Well, the street lights in Oakwood Avenue are not working. I was walking down there last night and it was very dark. It's dangerous. Someone will fall in the dark and get hurt. I think you should go there and have a look at the street lights.'

'And you want to go up in the inspection cradle to have a look at them too,' said Gordon with a laugh. 'Only council workers are allowed to go up in the inspection cradle, you know.'

'Give me a council worker's jacket and a safety helmet. No one will know I am not a council worker.'

At half past eight on Tuesday morning, Gordon drove the maintenance lorry out onto the street. Terry was sitting beside him in the lorry. He was wearing a council worker's jacket and a yellow safety helmet. When they got to Oakwood Avenue, Terry climbed onto the back of the lorry. He got into the inspection cradle. He carefully raised the cradle up to the top of the first lamp-post. Terry pretended to look at the street light and then spoke on his radio.

'All OK. Move onto the next lamp-post.'

The third lamp-post was opposite the garden gate of Number 12. Terry spoke again into the radio.

'There is something wrong with this lamp. I'm going to have a closer look.'

Terry moved the cradle over the front garden. It came nearer and nearer to the top floor of Number 12. Terry was able to look into the front bedroom.

Yes, Sheila was right. There was someone in the bed. It looked like a woman. And it looked as if she was dead. Terry got near enough to knock on the window. The woman wasn't dead. She sat up slowly in the bed and looked at Terry. Then she held her hands together as if she was praying. Terry knew she was asking him to help her.

Suddenly Terry looked down. Mr Jones had come out of the front door. Terry moved the cradle away from the bedroom.

Gordon drove the lorry slowly down to the next lamp-post. Mr Jones came out onto the road and turned away from the lorry. Mr Jones was carrying a small suitcase. Was he leaving town? Was he leaving the woman to die in the bedroom? Or was someone in the house with her?

When Mr Jones had gone round the corner of Oakwood Avenue, Terry spoke again into the radio. He told Gordon to drive back slowly to Number 12. He moved the cradle close up beside the window. There was a white face at the window. It was the woman. She had got out of bed and was standing at the window. She was trying to open the window, but it would not open.

Terry tried to open the window from the outside, but it was locked. He suddenly had an idea. There were some pieces of paper lying in the cradle. He quickly wrote a message in large letters.

ARE YOU IN TROUBLE? DO YOU WANT HELP?

The woman nodded her head up and down. Yes, she was in trouble. Yes, she wanted help.

Suddenly she waved her hands. She wanted Terry to go away. Someone was coming into the room. Terry moved the cradle away from the house.

Then he asked Gordon to drive the lorry out of Oakwood Avenue and round into Manor Park Road. They drove down

He quickly wrote a message in large letters.

Manor Park Road until they were opposite the back of 12 Oakwood Avenue. Terry again raised the inspection cradle high in the sky so that he could look into the garden of Number 12.

Yes. Tom Matthews had been right. There was a deep hole at the edge of some bushes. It was a grave and someone was going to be buried in it!

14

Mr Jones Goes to London

On Tuesday morning at half past nine, Mr Jones left Number 12 on important business. He had been giving Nancy morphine for five weeks. He knew she was very weak and ill, but she had not died.

Jones had a problem. He was unable to kill a woman. They had to die. Then no one could say that he had killed them. But there was no more morphine left. If he stopped giving the woman morphine, she would get stronger and would become well again. He had to get some more morphine.

He had got morphine before. It was quite easy. Jones went by train to London. On the train, he went into the toilet. He put make-up and some white powder on his face. Mr Jones now looked a sick man. When he got to London, he stayed in a small hotel near Piccadilly Circus. He told the manageress he did not feel very well. And the woman believed him. He looked pale and ill.

Jones waited until evening. Then he drank a large glass of water in which he had put a lot of salt. He waited for ten minutes and then he began to feel very sick.

He walked slowly down the stairs and asked the manageress to help him.

'Get a doctor, please,' he said. 'I don't feel well and I'm in terrible pain.'

When the woman saw him, she thought he was going to die. She phoned a doctor who came straight away.

'I'm very ill,' Henry Jones told the doctor. 'I do not have long to live. I'm in terrible pain.'

'Why don't you go to your own doctor?'

'My doctor is in Bristol,' replied Jones. 'I'm in London on business. I'm going back to Bristol next week. I need a drug that will stop my pain until then.'

The doctor looked at Jones and listened to his heart. Henry's face was white and there was sweat on his skin. The doctor saw that Henry was in great pain.

The doctor knew that he should phone Jones' doctor in Bristol. But that would take time and the doctor was extremely busy. He had very many patients to see that night. He quickly wrote out a prescription[26] and gave it to Jones.

This was what Jones was hoping the doctor would do. He knew that the doctors in central London were always very busy. That's why Jones had come to London.

Jones looked at the prescription. It was what he wanted. It was a prescription for morphine.

Jones knew that there was a chemist's[27] in Piccadilly that was open all night. It was one of the busiest chemist's shops in Britain.

Jones had to wait a long time before he was served. Lots of people were getting medicine with prescriptions. But Jones was not worried. There were so many people in the chemist's shop that no one would remember him.

After forty minutes, Mr Jones walked out of the chemist's. He now had all the morphine he needed. It was more than enough for Miss Nancy Roberts. She would die soon.

The doctor wrote out a prescription.

15

Terry Does Some Shopping

Terry was now sure that the woman in the upstairs bedroom at 12 Oakwood Avenue needed help. He had a plan to get her out.

He looked in the phone book. He found the name and address of a shop where he could hire theatrical costumes[28]. Terry knew what he was going to do. He had to get a fireman's uniform and some smoke bombs. He needed them in order to get into 12 Oakwood Avenue.

Terry caught a train to London and did some shopping. It was half past three when he got back to Beckenham. He left a box and a large bag in his office. Then he went to find Bill Evans.

'I need some more help from you and Tom,' he told the milkman. 'Can you find Tom and bring him with you to my office?'

Bill promised to be at Terry's office in half an hour.

16

Fire at Number 12

At half past seven on Wednesday morning, Tom arrived at Terry's office. He took all the newspapers out of his bag and laid them on the table. He picked up a box and put it in his bag. Then he got on his bicycle and rode to Oakwood Avenue.

Bill was waiting at Oakwood Avenue. He had stopped his milkfloat beside a telephone box at the end of the avenue. He looked at his watch. When it was eight o'clock exactly, he went into the phone box and dialled 999 for the emergency services. A woman's voice asked, 'Do you want police, fire or ambulance?'

'Fire,' replied Bill.

Then he heard a man's voice.

'Where are you calling from?'

'I'm calling from the telephone box at the end of Oakwood Avenue – near Manor Park Road,' said Bill. 'There's a fire at Number 12. I can see lots of smoke coming from the house.'

'12 Oakwood Avenue,' said the fireman. 'OK. Wait where you are. We'll be there in two minutes.'

Bill did not wait. He drove his milkfloat up the Avenue towards Number 12. After one minute, he sounded the horn of his milkfloat.

Suddenly smoke rose up in the garden of Number 12. Tom hid in the smoke and walked quietly up to the front door of Number 12. He pushed one smoke bomb through the letterbox and then another. Thick smoke began to come out of Number 12. It looked as if the house was on fire.

In a few minutes, the fire engine arrived. The firemen ran up to the door of Number 12 and began to beat on the door. A fireman came out from the side of the house where he had been waiting.

After a few moments, a woman opened the door of Number 12. She stood in the doorway coughing. Two firemen pushed past her into the house. Then a third fireman came running up the steps and pushed past her. The third fireman was carrying a sharp fireman's axe.

When he was inside the house, Terry knew where to go. He ran up the stairs to the second floor. The door of the front bedroom was locked. Terry raised the axe and brought it down on the door with all his strength. The door broke open. Yes, there was a woman on the bed. Terry picked up the woman in his arms.

43

He ran down the stairs. He had to get her out of the house as quickly as possible.

When the smoke had gone, the firemen saw that there had not been a fire at all.

'Someone has put a smoke bomb in here,' said one of the firemen. 'The police will be here soon. They'll want to have a look at this.'

At that moment, Terry reached the hallway carrying the woman. He walked outside. Two firemen looked at him in surprise.

'Wait a moment! Who are you?' one of the firemen asked.

'Stop! Stop!' shouted Isobel. 'That is a sick woman. She must not be moved.'

'No! No!' said the woman. 'I must get out of this house. They are keeping me here. They are going to murder me.'

The firemen could not believe what they had heard. What was happening?

Terry pulled off his fireman's helmet.

'It's me, Terry Mason,' he said. 'This is Miss Peters. She's been kept here a prisoner in her own house. She is very sick and we must get her to hospital as quickly as possible.'

'Terry Mason,' said one of the firemen. 'The private investigator! What are you doing here? Why are you pretending to be a fireman? That's against the law!'

Bill pushed past the people standing in front of Number 12. He walked over to Terry and took the woman in his arms.

'This is not Miss Peters!' Bill said. 'I've never seen this woman before.'

When Terry heard the words, 'not Miss Peters', he was very worried. Who was this woman? Had he made a terrible mistake? Was this Mr Jones' wife?

But when Isobel heard the words, 'Miss Peters', she ran down the steps of Number 12 towards the street.

She ran straight into a policeman.

'Wait a moment! Who are you?'

'What's happening here?' he asked.

'That's the man you should ask,' said Terry, pointing behind the policeman.

The policeman turned round and saw Mr Jones.

Mr Jones had been surprised when he saw the crowd in front of Number 12. He wanted to find out what was happening. He pushed his way to the front of the crowd. When he saw Isobel running away, he turned and started to run away too.

A police car arrived in Oakwood Avenue. It stopped quickly when the driver saw a man running away. A policeman jumped out, caught Mr Jones and held him.

While everyone was looking along the street, Terry quickly pulled off the fireman's uniform and hid it behind his back.

'This woman is not well,' Terry said to the policeman. 'We must get her to hospital!'

One of the policemen spoke into his radio.

'There's an ambulance on its way,' he said to Terry. 'Now Mr Mason, Mr Private Investigator, can you tell us what you are doing here?'

'That man and that woman will tell you everything,' said Terry, pointing to Mr Jones and his sister.

17

Where is Miss Peters?

An ambulance arrived and Nancy Roberts was carried inside. She turned to Terry and thanked him for his help.

'You have saved my life,' she said.

The police took Mr Jones and his sister to the police station. Terry and Bill also went to the police station.

'You have saved my life.'

Terry told the police about Sheila hearing the voice in the upstairs bedroom of Number 12. He told them what Bill, the milkman, had said.

'I thought that the woman in the upstairs bedroom was Miss Peters,' he said. 'I thought she was being kept prisoner in her own house. And when I heard that the man was digging a grave in the back garden, I thought it was a grave for Miss Peters.'

'So who is this woman? And where is Miss Peters?' asked the policeman.

'That's for you to find out,' said Terry. 'I've done my work. you have to do the rest.'

'Right,' said the policeman. 'Let's start digging.'

The police dug all day in the garden of Number 12, but they found nothing.

Also the police learnt very little from Mr Jones and his sister.

'I haven't murdered anyone. They died, but I didn't murder them,' Mr Jones said over and over again.

By the evening, Nancy Roberts was able to tell the police her story. She told them how she had met Isobel and her brother in Eastbourne. How she had got married in Hastings and then come with them to Beckenham. She told them how she had been kept locked in the upstairs bedroom. She thought that she had been given drugs to make her sleep all the time.

The police searched Number 12, but they didn't find any drugs. But when they searched Mr Jones' suitcase, they found the tablets of morphine. They arrested Jones and his sister. But they had not found out anything about Miss Peters. Where was she?

18

Sheila Has an Idea

That evening, Terry went to The Eight Bells as usual. There was a cheer when he walked through the door of the pub. Everyone had read the newspaper. They had seen the words on the front page: "You saved my life".

Terry was now famous. There were no more jokes about Sherlock Holmes. He was a hero.

But there was one person who was not pleased with Terry. Sheila was sitting in the pub looking very angry.

'This was my case,' said Sheila. 'It was me who started it all. And you left me out at the end. Why didn't you tell me what you were planning to do? I would have helped you.'

'But you laughed at me,' said Terry.

Sheila had to agree that she had laughed at Terry. Then they both had a good laugh and became friends again.

'Where is Nancy Roberts now?' Sheila asked Terry.

'In the hospital.'

'Let's go and see how she is,' said Sheila.

Terry thought that was a good idea and they both went to the hospital.

Nancy was feeling much better. She thanked Terry again and again.

'They were planning to murder me. I'm sure of that,' Nancy told them. 'They planned it all from the beginning. But you stopped them. You saved my life.'

Sheila then asked her about Miss Peters. But Nancy had never heard of her.

'Before he came to Eastbourne, Jones had some business to do in Brighton,' said Nancy. 'Then after the New Year holiday, he had some more business in Hastings. That's where we were married.'

'They are all towns on the south coast,' said Sheila.

'Yes,' agreed Nancy. 'They're all on the south coast and they are all quite near to each other.'

'First he's in Brighton. Then he's in Eastbourne. And finally Hastings. Doesn't that make you think?' Sheila said to Terry.

'Think what?' asked Terry.

'They are all holiday resorts. They are all places where nobody knows who you are. It would be easy for a man to get married to one woman in Brighton and then to another woman in Hastings.'

'That's an idea,' said Terry. 'I could go to Brighton and look at the marriage register there.'

'But who is paying for this?' asked Nancy.

'Well, usually, a private investigator works for a client,' replied Terry.

'Right,' said Nancy. 'I'm your client. You are working for me. I want you to find out more about Mr Jones. I want to know if he is my husband. If he is already married to Miss Peters, he can't be married to me.'

'Unless Miss Peters was dead before he married you,' said Sheila.

Terry went down to Brighton the next day. It did not take him long to find out that Henry Jones had been married to Miss Peters in August the year before. And one of the witnesses was Miss Isobel Jones.

But where was Miss Peters? That question still had to be answered. Terry looked at the addresses given in the marriage register. The address for Miss Peters was a hotel in Brighton. But for Mr Jones, there was an address in Canterbury. It was the same as the one Henry Jones had given in the marriage register.

Terry went by train to Canterbury. It did not take him long to find the house which Jones had given as his address. He rang the bell, but there was no reply.

Terry walked round to the back of the house. It had a large garden at the back. Thick bushes grew all round the sides. Terry walked round the garden slowly looking at the ground carefully. He found what he was looking for.

Yes, he was sure of it. A hole had been dug under some bushes and the ground had been covered with leaves. The police were digging in the wrong place. They were digging in the garden at 12 Oakwood Avenue. They should be digging for the body of Miss Peters here in this garden in Canterbury.

19

'Am I Married or Not?'

Miss Peter's body was found buried in the garden in Canterbury. Once again Terry's name was in the newspapers. But this time Sheila's name was there too. In an interview with a reporter, Terry said that it was Sheila who had given him the idea which made him go to Canterbury.

Nancy Roberts was now much better. Sheila and Terry found her sitting up in a chair when they went to visit her in hospital.

Nancy was horrified when Terry told her what he had discovered. She now knew what Jones had been planning to do to her. If Terry and Sheila had not investigated 12 Oakwood Avenue, she would now be in a grave in the garden.

'But if Miss Peters was dead before he married me, then I am still Jones' wife,' Nancy said, with horror in her voice.

'I don't think you are married to Henry Jones,' said Terry. 'I found out something interesting when I was in Brighton. I went to the hotel where Isobel Jones had stayed. There was no *Miss*

Isobel Jones in the hotel register. But there was a *Mrs* Isobel Jones. I don't think she is Jones' sister. I think she is his wife! I've told the police. I'm sure they'll find out that they are husband and wife.'

———

The trial of Henry Jones and his wife Isobel was front page news.

MORPHINE MURDERER ON TRIAL

The trial of Henry Jones and his wife Isobel came to an end yesterday. The two were found guilty of murdering Miss Angela Peters of 12 Oakwood Avenue and of the attempted murder of Miss Nancy Roberts of Cheltenham.

They were sentenced to life imprisonment. Terry Mason, a private Investigator, was thanked for the help he gave to the police.

POINTS
FOR
UNDERSTANDING

Points for Understanding

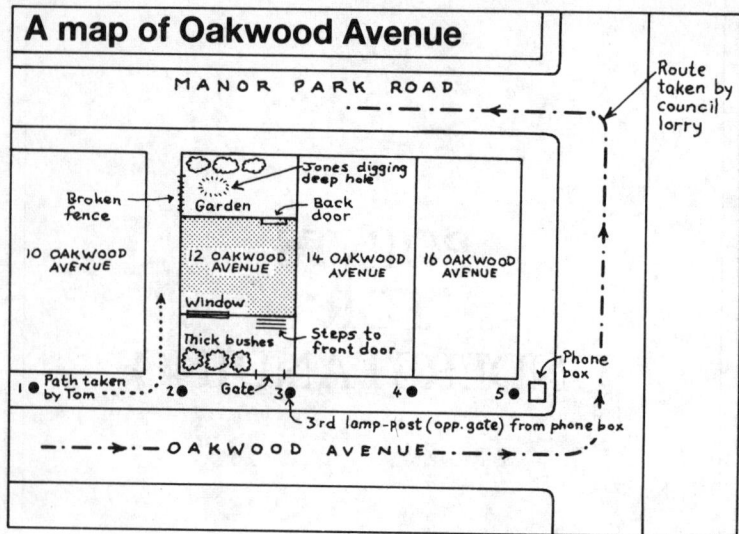

A map of Oakwood Avenue

MANOR PARK ROAD

Route taken by council lorry

Jones digging deep hole

Broken fence

Garden

Back door

10 OAKWOOD AVENUE

12 OAKWOOD AVENUE

14 OAKWOOD AVENUE

16 OAKWOOD AVENUE

Window

Thick bushes

Steps to front door

Phone box

Path taken by Tom

1 • 2 • Gate 3 • 4 • 5 □

3rd lamp-post (opp. gate) from phone box

OAKWOOD AVENUE

1

1 How old was Nancy Roberts when her father died?
2 Where did Nancy decide to have a holiday? Why?
3 What was Nancy afraid of?

2

1 Nancy made friends with Isobel Jones.
  (a) What did they decide to do?
  (b) Who was Isobel waiting for?
2 How did the love affair between Henry and Nancy Roberts start?

3

1 Why do you think Isobel left Nancy and Henry alone on Christmas Day?
2 Who was going to live with Henry and Nancy after they got married?
3 Why was Nancy not to tell anyone about the engagement?

4

1 Why was Henry going alone to Hastings?
2 Why was Nancy not to tell anyone about their plans?
3 What was Nancy going to tell the hotel manager?
4 Why could Nancy and Isobel not stay in the same hotel as Henry in Hastings?
5 What did Nancy do while she was in Hastings?
6 Henry and Nancy were married quietly.
    (a) Who were the witnesses?
    (b) What did they do after the wedding?

5

1 Why did Henry not get into the same taxi as Nancy and Isobel?
2 They walked quickly down a quiet, empty street.
    (a) Describe the house they stopped in front of.
    (b) What number was painted on the gate?
3 How did Nancy feel after she had drunk some coffee?
4 Why did Isobel say Nancy must stay in bed?
5 Did Henry come to see Nancy?
6 Nancy realised what a fool she had been. Why had Nancy been a fool?
7 Nancy heard two people pass by the house every morning. Who were they?
8 Nancy suddenly knew what was happening.
    (a) What was happening?
    (b) What did Nancy do?

6

1 What was Sheila Williams' work? Did she like it?
2 Why did Terry Mason not like his work?
3 Why did Terry dream of becoming a detective?
4 How was Terry able to become a detective?
5 Sheila thought Terry was mad. Why?
6 'Then I heard it.'
    (a) What did Sheila hear?
    (b) Where was she at the time?
    (c) What did she do?
    (d) What did Terry decide to do?

7

1 'You've got an appointment on Monday afternoon, Mr Smith.'
    (a) Who was Mr Smith?
    (b) What was the appointment?
2 Why did Terry go running?
3 Terry asked Bill Evans about Number 12.
    (a) Who was Bill Evans?
    (b) Who was Miss Peters?
    (c) How old was she?

8

1 Mr Jones told Sheila he was not married. Who did he say he lived with?
2 If there was a mortgage on Number 12, Bob Wilkinson could help Terry. How?

9

1 How did Terry find out that Miss Peters had been married to Mr Jones?
2 What did Sheila do when she was alone in the bedroom?
3 Why did Mr Jones tell Sheila and Terry to get out of the house?

10

1 Why could Henry and Isobel not leave an empty house?
2 'Perhaps she's dead,' said Isobel.
    (a) Who is 'she'?
    (b) What had Henry given her?
    (c) Why did Isobel not argue with Henry?

11

1 What did Terry find strange about Number 12?
2 What did Sheila find strange?
3 Where did Terry want to have a look?
4 'I've got an idea,' said Terry. Why would Terry not tell Sheila what his idea was?

12

1 What had Tom seen in the garden of Number 12?
2 What did Terry decide he was going to do?

13

1 What was Gordon Burgess responsible for?
2 How did Terry get a look into the bedroom?
3 How did Terry know that the woman in the bedroom wanted help?
4 Who did Terry see leaving Number 12?
5 What did Terry see in the garden?

14

1 Mr Jones told a doctor he was very ill.
    (a) What did he tell the doctor he needed?
    (b) Where had he left his medicine?
    (c) What did the doctor do?
2 Where did Mr Jones take the prescription?

15

1 Why did Terry want to hire a fireman's uniform?

16

1 What telephone number did Bill phone?
2 What did Tom put through the letterbox at Number 12?
3 How was Terry able to get into Number 12?
4 Why did Terry think he had made a terrible mistake?

17

1 What did the police find:
    (a) in the garden at Number 12?
    (b) in Mr Jones' briefcase?

18

1 Why was Sheila not pleased with Terry?
2 Why did Sheila think Terry should go to Brighton?
3 Why did Nancy want to know more about Mr Jones?
4 What did Terry find at Canterbury?

19

1 Why was Terry sure that Nancy was not married to Henry Jones?
2 What happened at the trial?

GLOSSARY

Glossary

1 **retired** (page 6)
most people retire from work when they become old. In Britain, women retire at sixty and men retire at sixty-five.

2 **left** – *had left (her money)* (page 6)
before Nancy's parents died, they signed papers to say that Nancy was to have their money.

3 **resort** – *holiday resort* (page 7)
a town where people go to spend their holidays. A holiday resort is often beside the sea.

4 **shy** (page 8)
a shy person is someone who does not make friends easily.

5 **affair** – *love affair* (page 10)
when two people fall in love, they have a love affair.

6 **quietly** (page 13)
only a few people are present at a quiet wedding.

7 **office** – *registry office* (page 13)
each large town and city in England has an office where people can get married.

8 **witness** (page 13)
at least two extra people must be present at a wedding. These two people must sign the register. They write their names in a book to say they have been present and they are the witnesses.

9 **poison** (page 16)
to do harm to someone by putting something bad in their food or drink.

10 **milkman** (page 16)
in England the milkman brings – delivers – milk and other things to houses every morning. The milkman carries these things on a milkfloat – a van driven by electricity. The newspaper boy brings newspapers.

11 **floor** (page 17)
the house at Number 12 Oakwood Avenue has four levels. The kitchen is in the basement which is below ground level. The sitting-room and dining-room are on the ground floor. The bedrooms where Henry and Isobel Jones sleep are on the first floor. And the bedroom where Nancy is kept a prisoner is on the second floor.

12 **building society** (page 18)
building societies are companies which lend money to people so that they can buy houses.

13 **estate agent** (page 18)
estate agents help people to buy and sell houses.

14 **solicitor** (page 19)
a solicitor is a lawyer. One of his/her jobs is to help people arrange who gets their money after they die.

15 **rent** (page 19)
when you rent something – a car or an office – you pay money for it every week or every year. The thing you rent never belongs to you.

16 **advert** (page 19)
if you want people to know that you are working as a private investigator, you put an advert – a notice – in a newspaper.

17 **house** – *to show someone round a house* (page 20)
Mr Jones wants to sell his house. Sheila comes to see the house and Mr Jones takes her into all the rooms – he shows her round the house.

18 **pretended** (page 21)
Sheila heard a noise, but she does not say anything to Mr Jones. She pretends that she did not hear the noise.

19 **case** (page 21)
a piece of business done by a detective is called a case.

20 **mortgage** (page 25)
a mortgage is a loan given by a building society (see Glossary no. 12) in order to buy a house.

21 **confidential** (page 26)
confidential information must be kept secret and not told to anyone.

22 **suspicious** (page 29)
people become suspicious when they think that someone is doing something wrong or against the law.

23 **tablets** – *morphine tablets* (page 31)
morphine is a very strong medicine which sick people take to stop them feeling pain. Morphine tablets can only be used when ordered by a doctor. If anyone takes too many tablets of morphine, they will die. Mr Jones crushes the tablets into a powder so that Nancy will not notice them in her food.

24 **arrested** (page 32)
a person who does something wrong is a criminal. A policeman's job is to catch – to arrest – criminals.

25 **maintenance** – *street lighting maintenance* (page 36)
in all towns and cities in Britain, local councils are responsible for
keeping the street lighting in good order. The lights must be
inspected – looked at carefully – from time to time. This is done by
workers who stand in a cradle and raise themselves high in the air. All
maintenance workers must wear safety helmets. See illustration on
page 38.

26 **prescription** – *write out a prescription* (page 40)
many medicines canot be bought unless the name and the amount of
medicine is written on a paper by a doctor. This paper is called a
prescription.

27 **chemist's** (page 40)
a shop where you can buy medicine.

28 **costumes** – *hire theatrical costumes* (page 42)
people acting in plays often want to wear special clothes – costumes.
For example, some actors might want to be dressed like soldiers or
sailors. There are shops in large cities in Britain where you can hire or
rent (see Glossary no. 15) such costumes. In these shops you can also
buy other things you need for a play, for example, bombs which make
a lot of smoke to look like fire.

Shane *by Jack Schaefer*
Old Mali and the Boy *by D. R. Sherman*
Bristol Murder *by Philip Prowse*
Tales of Goha *by Leslie Caplan*
The Smuggler *by Piers Plowright*
The Pearl *by John Steinbeck*
Things Fall Apart *by Chinua Achebe*
The Woman Who Disappeared *by Philip Prowse*
The Moon is Down *by John Steinbeck*
A Town Like Alice *by Nevil Shute*
The Queen of Death *by John Milne*
Walkabout *by James Vance Marshall*
Meet Me in Istanbul *by Richard Chisholm*
The Great Gatsby *by F. Scott Fitzgerald*
The Space Invaders *by Geoffrey Matthews*
My Cousin Rachel *by Daphne du Maurier*
I'm the King of the Castle *by Susan Hill*
Dracula *by Bram Stoker*
The Sign of Four *by Sir Arthur Conan Doyle*
The Speckled Band and Other Stories *by Sir Arthur Conan Doyle*
The Eye of the Tiger *by Wilbur Smith*
The Queen of Spades and Other Stories *by Aleksandr Pushkin*
The Diamond Hunters *by Wilbur Smith*
When Rain Clouds Gather *by Bessie Head*
Banker *by Dick Francis*
No Longer at Ease *by Chinua Achebe*
The Franchise Affair *by Josephine Tey*
The Case of the Lonely Lady *by John Milne*

For further information on the full selection of
Readers at all five levels in the series, please refer
to the Heinemann Readers catalogue.

Heinemann English Language Teaching
A division of Reed Educational and Professional Publishing Limited
Halley Court, Jordan Hill, Oxford OX2 8EJ

OXFORD   MADRID   FLORENCE   ATHENS   PRAGUE
SÃO PAULO   MEXICO CITY   CHICAGO   PORTSMOUTH (NH)
TOKYO   SINGAPORE   KUALA LUMPUR   MELBOURNE
AUCKLAND   JOHANNESBURG   IBADAN   GABORONE

ISBN 0 435 27230 6

© John Milne 1990, 1992
First published 1990
This edition published 1992

Illustrated by Christopher Price
Typography by Adrian Hodgkins
Cover by Jamel Akib and Threefold Design
Typeset in 11/12.5 pt Goudy
by Joshua Associates Ltd, Oxford
Printed and bound in Malta by Interprint Limited

97 98 99 00 10 9 8 7 6 5